BEN SHAHN

Ben Shahn

BEN SHAHN

HIS GRAPHIC ART

Text by James Thrall Soby

GEORGE BRAZILLER, INC.

NEW YORK   1957

CONTENTS

Illustration (above) for the story "Still Waters"
by Charles Jackson, published in *Charm,*
July, 1955. Drawing, 9¾ x 6¼. Owned by
the artist.

ACKNOWLEDGEMENTS

The illustrations in this book were made from the originals in the collections of the following private collectors and institutions and are reproduced here by their courtesy. These loans are gratefully acknowledged.

Mr. Winslow Ames
Mr. and Mrs. Alan E. Brandt
Mrs. John L. Bunce
The Downtown Gallery, New York City
Mr. and Mrs. Lawrence A. Fleischman
Fogg Art Museum, Cambridge, Mass.
Frederick and Emily Genauer Gash
Edith Gregor Halpert
Mr. and Mrs. Ira Herbert
Dr. J. Cotter Hirschberg
Dr. and Mrs. Wilfred C. Hulse
Mrs. Jacob M. Kaplan
Mr. Jack Lawrence
William H. Lane Foundation, Leominster, Mass.
Mr. and Mrs. John McAndrew
Museum of Modern Art, New York City
Mr. and Mrs. Gilbert Pleet
Mr. and Mrs. James S. Schramm
Mr. Jacob Schulman
Mr. and Mrs. Harris B. Steinberg
M. J. Stewart
Helen and Herbert Valentine
Mr. William Ward
Mr. and Mrs. Martin L. Weiss
Mr. and Mrs. Jack E. Young

Grateful acknowledgement is also made to the following publishers for their courtesy in granting permission to reproduce pages from books published by them: Farrar, Straus & Cudahy, New York City; The Gehenna Press, Northampton, Mass.; New Directions, New York City; and Pantheon Books, New York City.

Thanks are also due Edith Gregor Halpert of The Downtown Gallery for her willing cooperation in the preparation of this book.

Ben Shahn

THE GRAPHIC ART OF BEN SHAHN NO LESS THAN HIS PAINTING HAS alternated between realism and heraldry, between acute observation with satirical overtones and lyric invention. Its spirit has been sometimes acid, sometimes unguent. This is not to say, of course, that his art is in any way divided. On the contrary, it constitutes a *parure* of the finest order; all of it is marked by compassion, and most of it is immensely skilled. It would be hard to think of an American artist whose signature is more his own. Shahn has only to touch pen or pencil to paper to make his personality felt as clearly as in the most ambitious of his paintings. Indeed, few painters in this country can claim to have achieved a body of work in the graphic arts which as consistently parallels their imagery in what are thought to be the graver media of tempera and oil.

There is a particular and special reason why this should be so. For a considerable period, especially during the late 1930's and the 1940's, Shahn's drawings were the backbone of his paintings in the most literal sense of the word. From Diego Rivera, with whom in 1933 he worked on the fresco *Man at the Crossroads,* commissioned for the RCA building in Rockefeller Center and later destroyed in a sad moment of political censorship, he learned the Renaissance technique of "pouncing" drawings directly onto the bare surface of panels on which he was about to paint in tempera. The technique consisted in applying his contours through perforated sheets of tracing or wrapping paper and, Shahn writes, "When in painting the drawing became obliterated, I could 'repounce' the drawings back onto the painting." In recent years Shahn has abandoned this transfer process. But he adds: "I still draw before and during a painting. . . . I start with some drawing and very often stop several times during a painting to draw some area . . . in this way clarifying those areas of the painting which seemed vague when I started."

In view of the unusually close identification between Shahn's drawing and his painting, it is no wonder that he has been a prolific graphic artist, creating posters, illustrations, drawings, and prints in great number and of remarkable quality. This is most of all true of his career during the past dozen years or more. Yet he has always drawn a good deal: his first one-man show in New York (1930) consisted of sketches and water-colors of African subjects; thereafter he soon completed ten lithographs to illustrate De Quincey's "Levana" from *Suspiria de Profundis* and twelve border illustrations for the Haggadah. But then for a considerable period he was absorbed in painting series of small gouache pictures on such celebrated social themes as the cases of Sacco-Vanzetti and Tom Mooney. He tells me that no drawings were made for the first series and that, though at one point he dreamed of making a thousand drawings of characters in the Mooney case who had not appeared in his gouaches, only thirty or forty of these drawings were executed and few have survived.

Still later, Shahn was busy completing his admirable murals for various government agencies, and drawing played a supplementary role. I remember that in 1947, while organizing the Shahn exhibition for the Museum of Modern Art, I had difficulty in finding completed drawings by the artist. He explained that once a year he took part in a bazaar for the benefit of a local charity in the town of Roosevelt, New Jersey, where he lived and still lives. Shahn's contribution consisted in setting up shop in a booth, where he made portrait sketches of visitors for some absurdly low price (I think it was fifty cents apiece). His customers were usually alarmed by the likenesses he produced and so, he said, "I used to give them one or two of my other drawings for good measure." The simple, generous story moved me very much. But at that frantic moment of search for an adequate group of finished drawings for Shahn's show, it brought me close to throttling him for the only time in our quite long and I hope untroubled friendship.

The early Shahn drawings were notable for their cryptic restraint and their blunt disavowal of any interest in fluency and grace. This was during the first years of the Depression, and Shahn was reacting violently against the esthetic preoccupations of most of the painters and draftsmen whose works he had seen here and on two trips to Europe in 1925 and 1927. In the early 1930's, with abstract art once again in the ascendant, especially in Paris, he had the courage to affirm his faith in storytelling and humanitarian protest. For his new-found aims, which reached their maturity in the Sacco-Vanzetti and Mooney series of gouaches, he adopted a harsh linear method whose vigor springs from its deliberate sacrifice of beguilement to emotional fervor and documentary truth. He had aligned himself with the satirical tradition which runs from Hogarth through Daumier to the early George Grosz. Some indication of his personal contribution to this estimable tradition may be gained from the 1952 drawing of Sacco and Vanzetti in which, with accuracy and conviction, he recaptured the quality of his linear style of twenty-odd years before. The drawing's dark accents are held in evocative balance with the pale areas of surrounding elision; the characterization of the martyred shoemaker and fish peddler is masterful and pierc-

Drawing commissioned by Edward R. Murrow and Fred W. Friendly for the film "Ambassador Satchmo," 1956, edited by Mili Lerner. 9¾ x 6⅛. Owned by the artist.

ing, as it was in the original gouache series of 1931–32. The distortions of form in relating the massive heads of Sacco and Vanzetti to their diminutive bodies, seem inevitable and profoundly felt.

Shahn's last important mural commission was for the main corridor of the present U.S. Department of Health, Education, and Welfare Building in Washington, D.C. It was commissioned by the Section of Fine Arts of the U.S. Treasury and completed in 1942. That same year Shahn began to design posters as a member of the graphic arts division of the Office of War Information. Only two of these posters were published and put to actual use. Nevertheless, it seems likely that Shahn's work for the O.W.I. refreshed his interest in graphic art as a separate vehicle of communication. At any rate, from 1943 date the *Girl Skipping* (page 34), as economical in contour and relieving mass as a fine Japanese print, and the *Girl Skipping Rope* (page 35), in which the intricate patterns of the painting by the same name have not yet been devised and the impact consists in the offbeat tension of pose between the two figures. Here, as so often in Shahn's art, the principal motif of a given painting is quite exactly defined in a preparatory drawing. *The Violinist* of 1947 (page 43) is an additional case in point; its figure is utilized in the tempera picture of the same subject and year, with only those diminutions of scale (especially in the handling of the violin) which color made necessary.

From 1944 through 1946 Shahn was active in the graphic arts division of the C.I.O., and in 1945 became its director. There can be little doubt that both his own posters for this labor organization and his advisory responsibility for the work of others, clarified and deepened his gifts as designer and draftsman. Yet we should never forget how thorough was Shahn's training as a graphic artist. From 1913 to 1917, when still in his teens, he worked as a lithographer's apprentice, and he supported himself by his skill in this trade most of the time until 1930. To this day Shahn has retained his love of the meticulous control of simulated appearances which was an absolute requirement of the commercial lithographer's profession. His drawing often has the autonomous vitality of lines put down by Paul Klee, one of the twentieth-century artists Shahn most admires. But it can also be as exact, condensed, and immune to forgery as the engraving on government currency. It is this duality of vision—the poet combining with the squinting precisionist—which gives Shahn's graphic art much of its power and fascination.

Architecture and the human figure—these have always been the complementary focal points of Shahn's absorption in the world of reality around him. Ever since the Sacco-Vanzetti paintings of 1931–32, in one of which the façade of a municipal building provides a telling foil to the three glum stalwarts of the Lowell Committee, he has often played figures against an appropriate but pungently stylized architectural setting. Observe, for example, the drawing called *Porch No. 1* (page 41). Here Shahn has relieved the sharp contours of the seated boy by massed crosshatching to define the screened window and door and by the black accents of the railing and doorknob. The sense of mood is all-pervading, and every detail counts to the utmost—the clapboards of the frame house, the webbing of the chair, the counterplay of expression and posture between the seated boy and the younger child who peers out the window, pensive and curious, whereas the older boy watches the street lethargically. The essence of weather, hour, and mood has always been important to Shahn. He suggests it by architectural detail no less evocatively than by human stance and activity. He suggests it even when architecture is remotely placed, as in the *Street Scene* of 1956 (page 105).

At times, of course, Shahn has concerned himself with architecture alone, as in the *Brick Building* and the *Brownstone Front* (pages 48 and 49), the one heavily constructed, with blackened windows and a rooftop fantasy of ventilators and stacks, the other defiant in its Victorian effulgence; the one seen head on and massive, the other twisted purposefully in the perspective of the railings and stairs. The idiosyncrasy of buildings and their humanistic allusions interest Shahn most. He frequently tells fortunes by the places people inhabit or in which they work. Could any image more poignantly express the dour life of miners than the dark *Mine Building* (page 69)?

As an artist Shahn seems to have no preference as to architectural materials so long as he tells the truth about each. In *May 5,* for example, wood, stone, and brick are given their separate character in the kind of unreasoning structural admixture of which the painter is fond. And in this image, as often in his work, a satirical point is made quietly, in this case by the billboard's lettering which assures a theater's potential audience that the actors will not be Negroes but white men in blackface. For this sort of racial injustice there is for now, I suppose, no adequate retribution, though Virgil Thomson came close to turning the scales by proposing (in vain) that the magnificent Negro cast of his opera *Four Saints in Three Acts* should perform in whiteface. But the moral of Shahn's satire is never labored and seldom overtly angered. His concern, as I wrote of him some years ago, is to thread protest through the needle of reality.

May 5. 1949. Tempera (original in color), 24 x 30.
Collection Mr. and Mrs. Edward F. Kook.

A large percentage of Shahn's graphic works, as I already suggested, portrays the human figure, with or without those inanimate accessories among which musical instruments play a role second only to architecture. The emotional and stylistic range of his drawings and watercolors of human subjects is altogether exceptional, alternating between caricatural humor and reflective solemnity. To the former category belongs the unforgettable cartoon of Truman and Dewey, executed during the political campaign of 1948. The two candidates, on whom Shahn obviously looked with equal suspicion, are ingeniously placed, Dewey atop a piano and Truman at its keyboard, before sheets of music whose titles are a vital part of the artist's satirical message and whose varied styles of printing attest Shahn's lifelong interest in typographical matters. Details are handled with remarkable acuteness: the strained cordiality of Dewey's smile, for example; the wrinkles in Truman's trousers and the amateurish flourish with which his right hand strikes a chord; the definition of both candidates' feet. Yet distortions and elisions are just as important, as in the aggrandizement of the two politicians' heads and the subtle way in which Truman's eyeglasses are left blank and the teeth of both men are frozen in bright evenness. This is an image intended to provoke laughter regardless of one's political convictions. I suspect it will take its place among the most effective caricatures of recent times.

(Above) *Truman and Dewey*. 1948. Watercolor (original in color), 37½ x 24½. The Downtown Gallery.

No less haunting as mirthful comment on contemporary mores is the wash drawing *Susanna and the Elders* (page 45). The sacrosanct title of the picture gives its modern vulgarity a particular cogency. The fat lecher in suspenders, one of his eyes quite literally popping out of his head, ogles a Coney Island temptress dressed in a ridiculous bra and transparent skirt, her vacuous face denying the elegance and beauty with which Susanna unwillingly tormented the Elders in the Apocryphal story. As a present-day transcription of the ancient episode, the drawing is a cartoon on a very high level, not at all irreverent, but wry and funny.

Shahn's gaiety and humor break through at intervals throughout his career, as though he had taken to heart Paul Klee's wise dictum: "There is a laughter which is to be put on the same dignified level as higher lyrical emotions, and which is as distant as heaven from the convulsions of a vulgar clown." Look, for instance, at the *Bicycle Act* of 1950 (page 53), in which the irrepressible acrobats are projected against harlequin banners, their feats of balance conveying a wonderful sense of abandon and motion. Here once more Shahn has proved his ability to reduce a complicated scene to deft essentials of line and contrast. One knows precisely what the cyclists are doing despite the fairly abstract nature of the overall design. Indeed, the fusion of abstraction with realism has been one of the artist's most commendable achievements in recent years. To understand the compulsive daring of the liberties he takes with reality, one need only study the colored silkscreen print entitled *Triple Dip* (page 66), wherein the cropped head and foreshortened left leg of the boy are uncommonly convincing.

As a humorist Shahn has long been interested in the temperamental extremes of rage and conviviality. The frenzied entanglement of the two fighting men in *Discord* (page 79) typifies one extreme, and in it may be seen at its clearest a favorite iconographical device of the painter—an upflung hand with stubby, strong fingers. The mood is opposite in *College Reunion* (page 90), a small drawing of aging celebrants, their mouths convulsed in song. One of his most recent drawings, the *Existentialists* of 1957 (page 123), illustrates a gamut from somber to insipid; the self-conscious seriousness of the three figures at the left is hopelessly compromised by the banal grin of their companion at the right. The hands of the figures are given a major expressive role, as so often in Shahn's paintings and graphic art.

"But most important," Shahn once remarked, "is always to have a play back and forth, back and forth. Between the big and the little, the light and the dark, the smiling and the sad, the serious and the comic." Hence, simultaneously with his humorous drawings, he has created works like the *Man Picking Wheat* (page 50), in which the atmosphere is quiet and thoughtful and the large figure is beautifully contrasted with the slender plants amid which he stands. As a painter and draftsman Shahn has seldom been concerned with landscape as such and for its own sake. He has turned his back on the wild, panoramic vistas which inspired our artists of the Hudson River School; he prefers details of urban parks and farm land. Indeed, he is essentially a painter of the city, and characteristically once declared that in the country, "every day is like Sunday." Yet of trees and plants and the flat terrain near Roosevelt, New Jersey, he has made intimate and evocative backdrops to his varied studies of the figure.

Some measure of his inventiveness in handling the figure may be had by comparing the *Drawing for "Mother and Child"* (page 77) with the *Portrait of Dr. J. Robert Oppenheimer* (page 87), the one tender and calm, the other ferocious in its reflection of the torment of uncompromising intelligence which haunted the great scientist in his moment of social ordeal (the drawing was executed in 1954 at the time of climax in Dr. Oppenheimer's political difficulties). Shahn had known Dr. Oppenheimer when the latter was Director of the Institute for Advanced Study at Princeton (which is near Roosevelt, New Jersey), and perhaps this accounts in part for the portrait's extraordinary reality and forcefulness. Even so, it would be hard to think of many contemporary portrait drawings, whether American or foreign, which have as hypnotic a strength of characterization.

Illustration for the story "Still Waters" by Charles Jackson, published in *Charm,* July, 1955. Drawing, 6 x 9¾. Owned by the artist.

A similar contrast of approach, as between *Drawing for "Mother and Child"* and the Oppenheimer portrait, may be felt in the two pictures called *Chicago* and the *Study for "Goyescas"* (pages 101 and 71). The drawing of a Chicago jazz band is a vivid and appealing record of the rapture of its musicians, bound together by rhythmic arabesques of heavy line. The surface arabesques reappear in the baseball drawing entitled *Safe* (page 103), wherein the exaggerated spikes on the base runner's shoes become a focal point of desperate exertion. Both the last-named drawings are amazingly effective in their suggestion of violent motion; both are marked by Shahn's affectionate regard for typically American subjects. But the artist's mood turns dark again in the superb *Study for "Goyescas,"* with its hideously triumphant officer holding aloft over the strewn corpses of his victims a cat's cradle of barbed wire. And the three images just mentioned typify among them the blend of laughter and horror which is an earmark of Shahn's compassion.

In a good number of Shahn's recent works, both paintings and drawings, there is a strong heraldic or symbolic content. It is difficult to make precise when this trend in his art became apparent for the first time. But the artist has told me of two contributory factors. The first of these was that in August, 1948, his illustrations for an article called "The Hickman Story" appeared in *Harper's Magazine*. The story described a famous and infamous tenement fire which had taken place in Chicago the year before and in which several of the Hickman children were killed. For Shahn the story evoked painful childhood memories. In 1909, when he was eleven, the house in which he lived with his family on Lorimer Street, Brooklyn, burned down at night, and the four Shahn children were saved at the last moment by their father, who dropped them out a window into the arms of a friend standing below. While working on the illustrations for "The Hickman Story," Shahn began to think of fire as a lion with flamelike mane. Gradually his interest in symbolism and allegory became more obsessive, and there followed the brilliant series of paintings and graphic works which includes the several versions of *Where There's A Book* (page 54), *Harpie* (page 65), and *Phoenix* (page 67). There followed, too, the two drawings of 1954 entitled *Alphabet* and *Second Alphabet* (pages 80 and 81), the one an astonishingly inventive arrangement of abstract, calligraphic forms, the other a severe and proud heraldic image.

The second factor Shahn has mentioned as contributing to the symbolic and allegorical connotations of much of his recent art, has been his desire to create Christmas cards and booklets which would avoid the sickly prettiness of commercial designs in this field. Perhaps even more important, however, has been his reading of the *Iliad* and of William Blake's prose and poetry, especially *The Marriage of Heaven and Hell*. At any rate, though never abandoning the quick and poetic transposition of reality evident in such drawings as *Silent Music* and *Television Antenna* (pages 56–57 and 74), and in his drawings for a projected book on the life of Louis Armstrong (pages 106–110), Shahn has broadened and made more profound the philosophical implications of his art during the past ten years. He has done so notably in his many studies for an ambitious painting called *Labyrinth*. His plastic scope now extends from the magic reportage of his sketches of a typewriter or a farm machine (pages 115 and 91) to the expressionism of *Drawing for "Labyrinth"* (page 62); from the delicacy of *Wheat* (end papers) to the ecstasy of *Bach* (pages 85 and 95) or the tense gravity of *Study for "The Marriage of Heaven and Hell"* (page 93).

The Marriage of Heaven and Hell! To Shahn might well be applied Swinburne's words on Blake's great book: "Passion and humour are mixed in his writing like mist and light; whom the light may scorch or the mist confuse it is not his part to consider."

Illustration (on facing page) for the story
"The Lilies" by Aldous Huxley, published in
Charm, July, 1953. Drawing, 6 x 5⅜. Owned
by the artist.

NOTES TO THE REPRODUCTIONS

The numbers preceding the reproductions refer to the page. Dimensions are given in inches; height precedes width.

ENDPAPERS: *Wheat.* 1955. Drawing, 25½ x 38½. Collection William H. Lane Foundation.

FRONTISPIECE: *Artist.* 1953. Drawing, 26 x 20. Collection Mr. and Mrs. John McAndrew.

PAGE

33 *Children of the Streets.* 1943. Drawing, 11⅞ x 9¼. Owned by the artist.

34 *Girl Skipping.* 1943. Drawing, 12 x 7. Collection Mr. and Mrs. James S. Schramm.

35 *Girl Skipping Rope.* 1943. Ink drawing, 22 x 30. Collection Mr. James Thrall Soby.

36 *Father and Child.* 1946. Tempera painting (original in color), 40 x 30. The Museum of Modern Art, gift of James Thrall Soby.

37 *Pounce drawing for "Father and Child."* 1946. Drawing, 39½ x 29. The Museum of Modern Art, gift of James Thrall Soby.

38 Detail of *Pounce drawing for "Father and Child."* (Original size.) 1946. Drawing, 39½ x 29. The Museum of Modern Art, gift of James Thrall Soby.

39 *Pounce drawing for "Father and Child."* 1946. Drawing, 29⅜ x 18⅝. The Museum of Modern Art, gift of James Thrall Soby.

40 One of a series of drawings done during a Southern trip. 1946. Drawing, 16 x 12. Owned by the artist.

41 *Porch #1.* 1947. Brush and ink drawing, 11½ x 16. Collection Dr. J. Cotter Hirschberg.

42 *Dancers*. 1947. Charcoal drawing, 24⅜ x 18. Collection Mrs. John L. Bunce.

43 *The Violinist*. 1947. Brush and ink drawing, 30 x 21½. Collection Mr. William Ward.

44 Study for the brochure "Eagle's Brood" issued by the Columbia Broadcasting System, November, 1947. Drawing, 16 x 13⅞. Owned by the artist.

45 *Susanna and the Elders*. 1948. Wash drawing, 22½ x 31½. Collection Mr. and Mrs. Alan E. Brandt.

46 *Vanity*. 1948. Ink drawing, 9⅝ x 6⅜. Collection Edith Gregor Halpert.

47 *Watermelon Eater*. 1949. Drawing, 40 x 27. Private Collection.

48 *Brick Building*. 1948. Tempera drawing, 32 x 23. Museum of Art, University of Michigan.

49 *Brownstone Front*. 1950. Drawing, 38 x 25. Carpenter Art Galleries, Dartmouth College.

50 *Man Picking Wheat*. 1950. Drawing, 38 x 25. Fogg Art Museum, Harvard University, Meta and Paul J. Sachs Collection.

51 Illustration for the article "On the Generalized Theory of Gravitation" by Albert Einstein, published in *Scientific American,* April, 1950. Drawing. Private Collection.

52 Illustration for the article "The Strangest Place in Chicago" by John Bartlow Martin, published in *Harper's Magazine,* December, 1950. Drawing, 9 x 6. Owned by the artist.

53 *Bicycle Act.* 1950. Drawing, 38 x 25. Collection Edith Gregor Halpert.

54 *Where There's a Book.* 1950. Drawing, 5½ x 7. The Downtown Gallery.
   Where There's a Book. 1950. Drawing, 16 x 12½. Collection Mr. Jacob Schulman.

55 *Cello with Chairs.* 1951. Drawing, 16 x 23. Collection Mr. and Mrs. James S. Schramm.

56–57 *Silent Music.* 1950. Silkscreen, 25½ x 38¾. The Downtown Gallery.

58 *Frog Monster.* 1951. Watercolor, 12 x 8½. Collection Mr. and Mrs. James S. Schramm.

59 *Homeric Struggle.* 1951. Drawing, 30½ x 25¼. The Downtown Gallery.

60–61 *Porch.* 1951. Drawing, 9 x 18. Collection Mr. and Mrs. Martin L. Weiss.

62 *Drawing for "Labyrinth."* 1952. Drawing, 14 x 11. Collection Mr. and Mrs. Gilbert Pleet.

63 *Sacco and Vanzetti.* 1952. Drawing, 8½ x 10. Fogg Art Museum, Harvard University, Meta and Paul J. Sachs Collection.

64 *Six.* 1952. Drawing, 39 x 25¼. Collection Mr. and Mrs. Herbert L. Cohen.

The following eight pictures are reproduced in full color.

65 *Harpie.* 1951. Gouache, 26¼ x 39¼. The Downtown Gallery.

66 *Triple Dip.* 1952. Theorem (silkscreen and color), 30¾ x 22½. The Downtown Gallery.

67 *Phoenix.* 1952. Theorem (silkscreen and color), 22¼ x 30¼. The Downtown Gallery.

68 *Porch with Two Figures.* 1953. Drawing and watercolor, 13½ x 25. Collection Mr. and Mrs. Ira Herbert.

69 *Mine Building.* 1956. Theorem (silkscreen and color), 22⅜ x 30¾. The Downtown Gallery.

Drawing commissioned by Edward R. Murrow and Fred W. Friendly for the film "Ambassador Satchmo," 1956, edited by Mili Lerner. 12 x 9½. Owned by the artist.

70 *Clown.* 1955. Watercolor, 38 x 25. The Downtown Gallery.

71 *Study for "Goyescas."* 1956. Watercolor, 25½ x 30. Collection M. J. Stewart.

72 *Lute #2.* 1957. Watercolor, 38¼ x 25. Collection Mr. and Mrs. Harris B. Steinberg.

73 Study for pamphlet "The Untouchables" issued by the Southern Conference Educational Fund, Inc., 1952. Drawing, 8⅞ x 6. Owned by the artist.

74 *Television Antenna.* 1952. Drawing, 31¼ x 22½. The Downtown Gallery.

75 Illustration for the story "The Lilies" by Aldous Huxley, published in *Charm,* July, 1953. Drawing, 6⅞ x 11⅞. Owned by the artist.

76 *Arch of Triumph.* 1953. Drawing, 22½ x 29½. The Downtown Gallery.

77 *Drawing for "Mother and Child."* 1953. Drawing, 8½ x 11¼. Collection Mr. and Mrs. Jack E. Young.

78 Illustration for the story "The Lilies" by Aldous Huxley, published in *Charm,* July, 1953. Drawing, 6 x 6½. Owned by the artist.

79 *Discord.* 1953. Drawing, 31½ x 25. The Downtown Gallery.

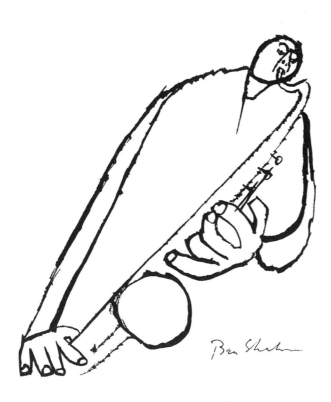

Drawing commissioned by Edward R. Murrow and Fred W. Friendly for the film "Ambassador Satchmo," 1956, edited by Mili Lerner. 8¾ x 8⅛. Owned by the artist.

80 *Alphabet.* 1954. Drawing, 36 x 25½. Fogg Art Museum, Harvard University, Meta and Paul J. Sachs Collection.

81 *Second Alphabet.* 1954. Drawing, 40 x 26. Joslyn Art Museum.

82 Illustration for the story "The Wonderful Death of Dudley Stone" by Ray Bradbury, published in *Charm,* July, 1954. Drawing, 9¾ x 6. Owned by the artist.

83 Double-page spreads from *The Alphabet of Creation* published by Pantheon Books, New York, 1954. The edition consisted of 50 copies numbered from 1 to 50, each including an original drawing by the artist, and 500 copies numbered from 51 to 550, all signed by the artist.

84 *Te Deum.* 1954. Drawing, 12 x 12½. Collection Mr. Jack Lawrence.

85 *Bach.* 1954. Drawing, 24 x 19½. Collection Mr. and Mrs. James S. Schramm.

86 Drawing for the story "A Matter of Adjustment" by Nadine Gordimer, published in *Charm,* March, 1954. Drawing, 9¾ x 24¼. Collection Helen and Herbert Valentine.

87 *Dr. J. Robert Oppenheimer.* 1954. Brush and ink drawing, 19½ x 12¼. The Museum of Modern Art.

88 *Study for "Maimonedes."* 1954. Drawing, 11½ x 9. Collection Frederick and Emily Genauer Gash.

89 *Blind Botanist.* 1954. Drawing, 38½ x 25½. Fogg Art Museum, Harvard University, Meta and Paul J. Sachs Collection.

90 *College Reunion.* 1954. Drawing, 10 x 6. Collection Mr. and Mrs. Lawrence A. Fleischman.

91 *Farm Machine.* 1955. Drawing, 18 x 12. The Downtown Gallery.

92 *Sad Clown.* 1955. Drawing, 11 x 8½. The Downtown Gallery.

93 *Study for "The Marriage of Heaven and Hell."* 1955. Watercolor, 35 x 25. Collection Mr. Jacob Schulman.

94 *Today is the Birthday of the World.* 1955. Drawing, 22½ x 31. Private Collection.

95 *Bach.* 1955. Drawing, 40 x 26. The Downtown Gallery.

96–97 *P. S. #3.* 1955. Drawing, 7½ x 11¾. The Downtown Gallery.

98 *Head of Lincoln.* 1955. Drawing, 12½ x 9½. The Downtown Gallery.

99 *Study for "Second Spring."* 1955. Drawing, 20⅜ x 15¾. Owned by the artist.

100 *Cafe.* 1955. Drawing, 24½ x 19½. Collection Mr. and Mrs. Lawrence A. Fleischman.

101 *Chicago.* 1955. Drawing, 26 x 39. The Downtown Gallery.

102 *National Pastime.* 1955. Drawing, 40¼ x 26¾. The Downtown Gallery.

103 *Safe.* 1956. Ink drawing, 27¼ x 40¼. The Downtown Gallery.

104 *African Porters.* 1956. Drawing, 12 x 9¼. Collection Mr. Winslow Ames.

105 *Street Scene.* 1956. Drawing, 25½ x 38½. The Downtown Gallery.

106–110 Drawings commissioned by Edward R. Murrow and Fred W. Friendly for the film "Ambassador Satchmo," 1956, edited by Mili Lerner.

111 Double-page spreads from *Thirteen Poems* by Wilfred Owen, published by The Gehenna Press, Northampton, Mass., 1956. Limited to 400 copies.

112–113 *Circus Tumblers.* 1956. Drawing, 24 x 33. The Downtown Gallery.

114 *The Owl.* 1956. Drawing, 29½ x 21. Private Collection.

Drawing commissioned by Edward R. Murrow and Fred W. Friendly for the film "Ambassador Satchmo," 1956, edited by Mili Lerner. 6¾ x 12. Owned by the artist.

115 Drawing for the article "Three Machines That Changed Everything: 2. The Typewriter" by Avis Manno, published in *Charm,* January, 1956. Drawing, 8¼ x 11¼. Collection Helen and Herbert Valentine.

116 *Skating Rink.* 1956. Drawing, 25½ x 38½. The Downtown Gallery.

117 Double-page spreads from *Homage to Mistress Bradstreet* by John Berryman, published by Farrar, Straus & Cudahy, New York, 1956.

118 *Negro Mother and Child.* 1956. Drawing, 12¼ x 9½. The Downtown Gallery.

119 *Freud.* 1956. Drawing, 31 x 22¼. Collection Mr. and Mrs. Lawrence A. Fleischman.

120 *Tablets of the Law with Lion.* 1956. Drawing, 32 x 22¾. Collection Dr. and Mrs. Wilfred C. Hulse.

121 *Triciput (After Titian).* 1956. Drawing, 22½ x 18. The Downtown Gallery.

122 *Priest and the Prophet.* 1957. Drawing, 38¼ x 25¼. Collection Mrs. Jacob M. Kaplan.

123 *Existentialists.* 1957. Drawing, 39 x 27. The Downtown Gallery.

124 Double-page spreads from *The Sorrows of Priapus* by Edward Dahlberg, published by New Directions, Norfolk, Conn., 1957. A limited edition of 150 copies, signed by the author and artist, and a trade edition.

125 *Helix.* 1957. Drawing, 40½ x 26½. The Downtown Gallery.

THE REPRODUCTIONS

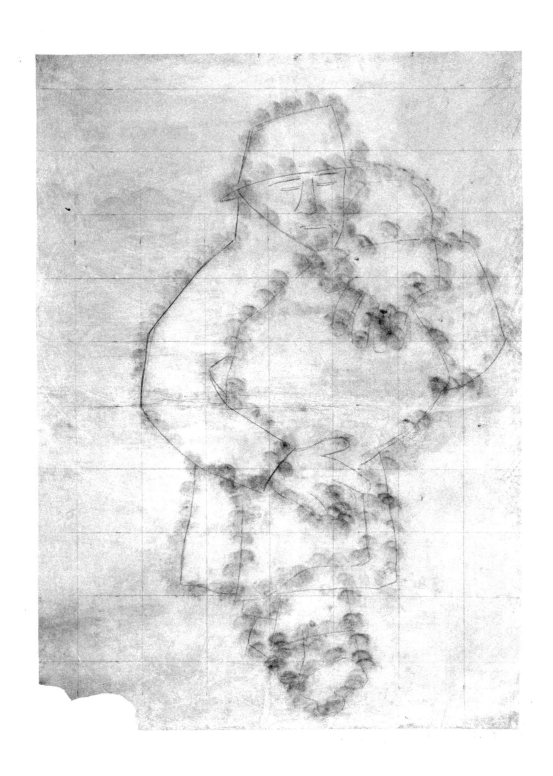

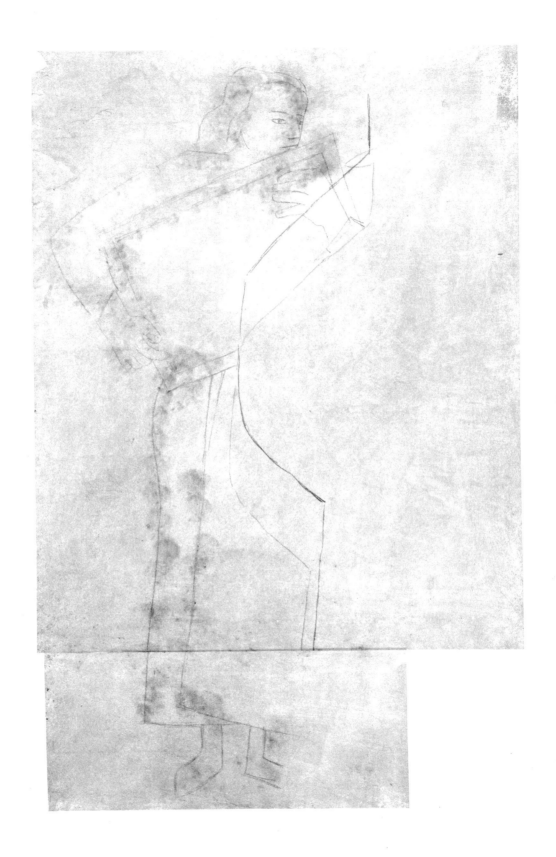

41

אַ סִ פֿ אַ

אַ פֿ סַ רֿ אַ

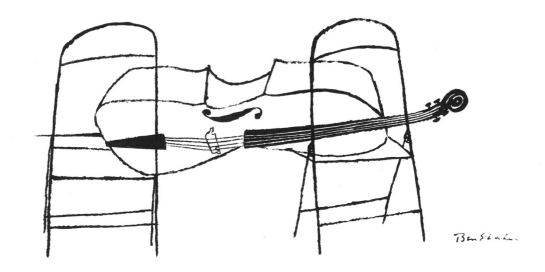

"If it had not been for these thing, I might have live out my life talking at street corners to scorning men. I might have die, unmarked, unknown, a failure. Now we are not a failure. This is our career and our triumph. Never in our full life could we hope to do such work for tolerance, for joostice, for man's onderstanding of man as now we do by accident. Our words — our lives — our pains nothing! The taking of our lives — lives of a good shoemaker and a poor fish peddler — all! That last moment belongs to us — that agony is our triumph." — *Bartolomeo Vanzetti*

66

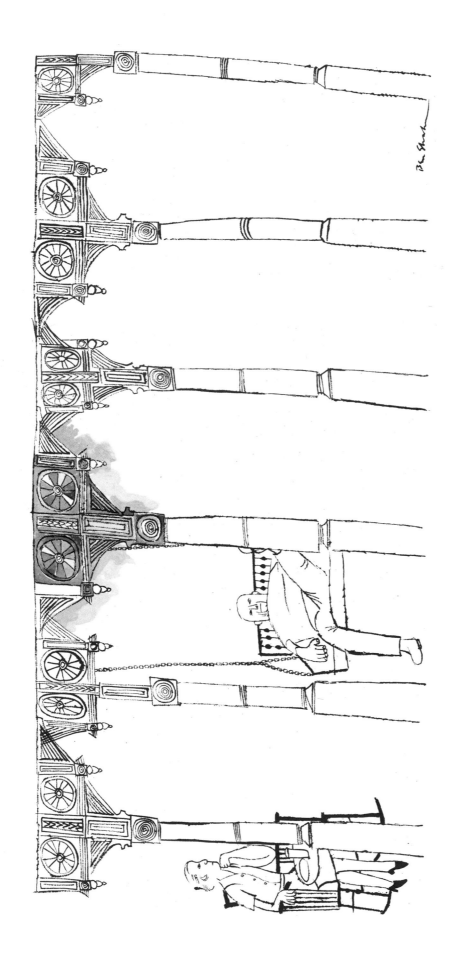

70

Ben Shahn

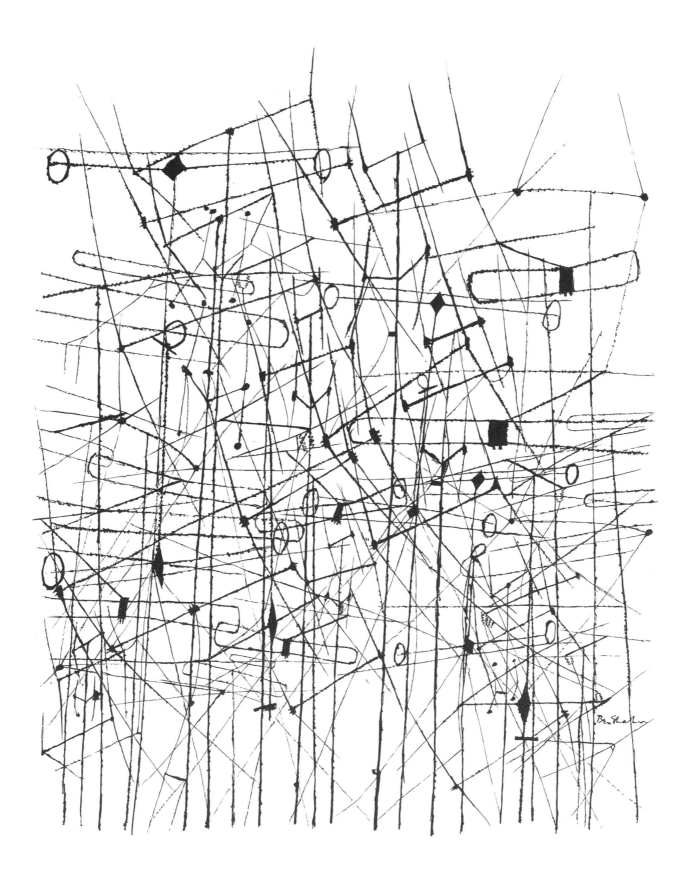

74

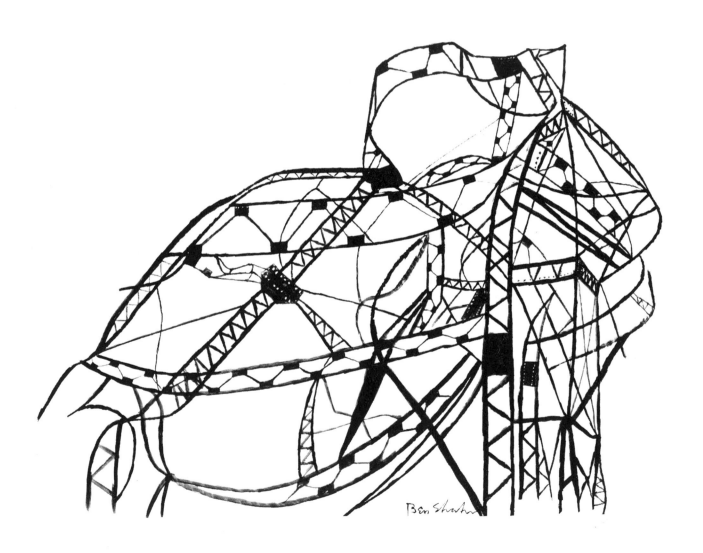

Thine own name, Shaddai, begins
with me!" But Shin was rejected
because it was his ill fortune to

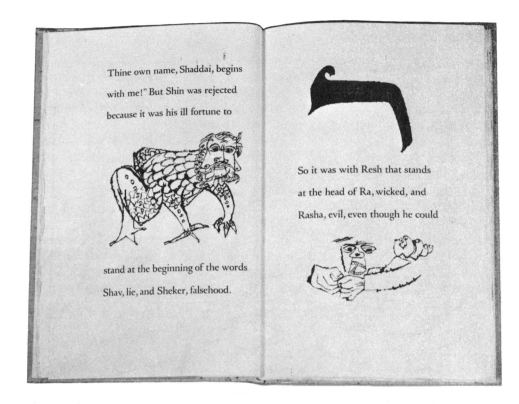

stand at the beginning of the words
Shav, lie, and Sheker, falsehood.

So it was with Resh that stands
at the head of Ra, wicked, and
Rasha, evil, even though he could

give praise unto Thee through me.
For it is said, 'Baruch—blessed—be
the Lord forever: Amen and

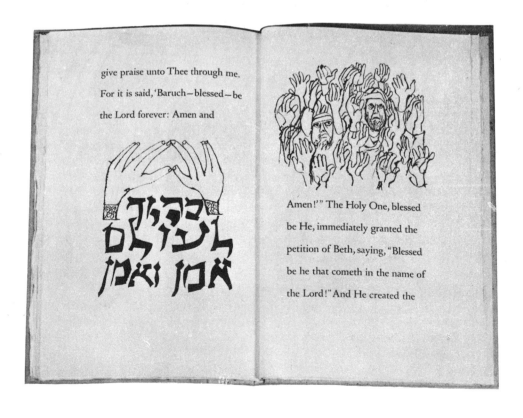

Amen!'" The Holy One, blessed
be He, immediately granted the
petition of Beth, saying, "Blessed
be he that cometh in the name of
the Lord!" And He created the

The Prophets Isaiah and Ezekiel dined
with me, and I asked them how they dared so
roundly to assert that God spoke to them, and
whether they did not think at the time that they
would be misunderstood, and be the cause of imposition.

Isaiah answer'd: "I saw no God, nor heard any, in a
finite organical perception; but my sense discover'd
the infinite in everything, and I was then persuaded,
and remain confirm'd, that the voice of honest
indignation is the voice of God. I cared not
for the consequences, but wrote."

Then I asked: "Does a firm perswation that a thing
is so, make it so?"

He replied: "All Poets believe that it does, and in
ages of imagination
this firm
perswation
removed mountains;
but many are
not capable of
a firm perswation of any thing."

William Blake

93

הינם זרת עלום

הינם יעמד במשפט כל יצורים אם כבנים אם כעבדים אם כבנים רחמנו כרחם אב על בנים ואם כעבדים עינינו לך תלויות עד שתחננו ותוציא כאור משפטנו איום קדוש.

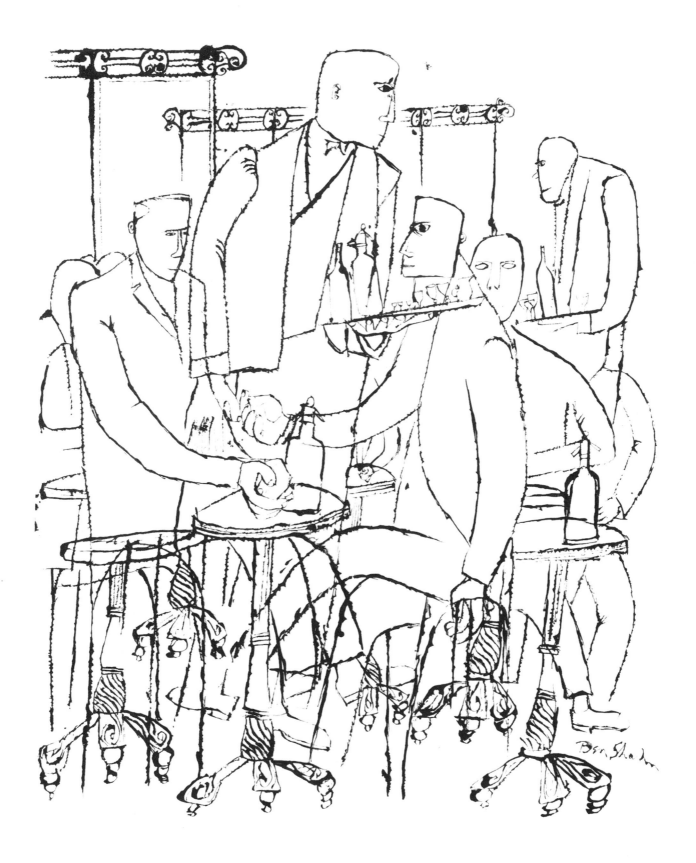

103

104

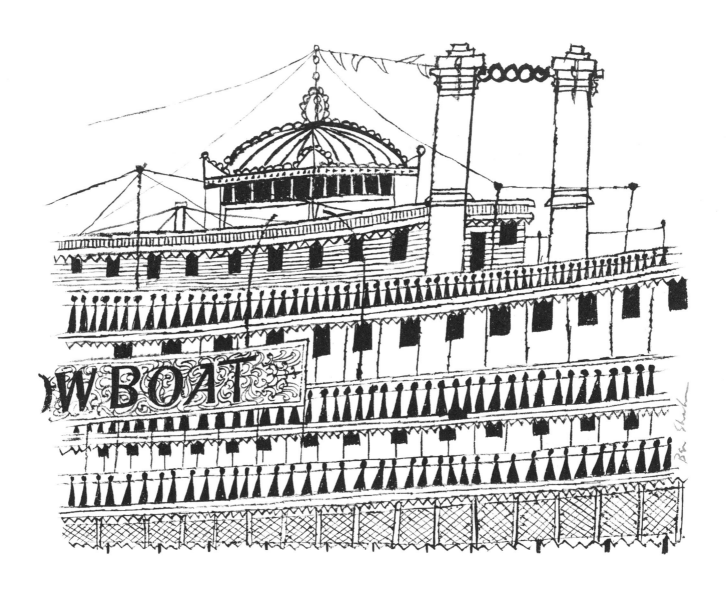

106

108

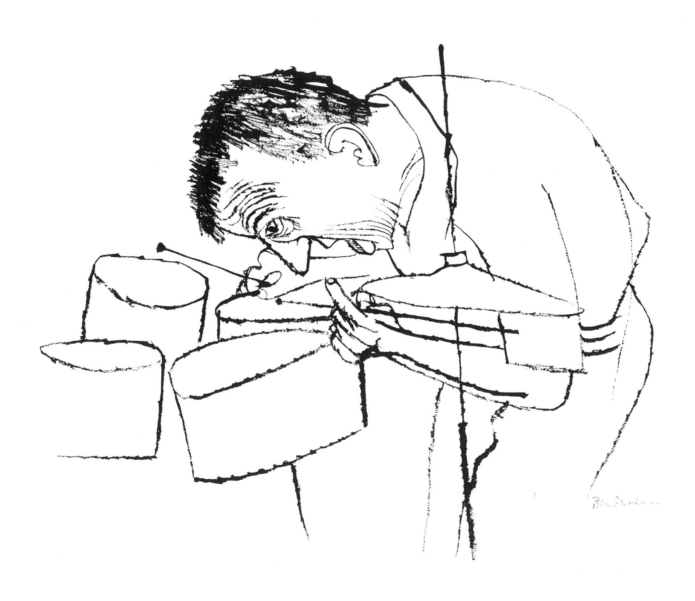

110

THE PARABLE OF THE OLD MEN
AND THE YOUNG

So Abram rose, and clave the wood, and went,
And took the fire with him, and a knife.
And as they sojourned both of them together,
Isaac the first-born spake and said, My Father,
Behold the preparations, fire and iron,
But where the lamb for this burnt-offering?
Then Abram bound the youth with belts and straps,
And builded parapets and trenches there,
And stretched forth the knife to slay his son.
When lo! an angel called him out of heaven,
Saying, Lay not thy hand upon the lad,
Neither do anything to him. Behold,
A ram, caught in a thicket by its horns;
Offer the Ram of Pride instead of him.
But the old man would not so, but slew his son,—
And half the seed of Europe, one by one.

I have perceived much beauty
    In the hoarse oaths that kept our courage straight;
    Heard music in the silentness of duty;
    Found peace where shell-storms spouted reddest spate.

Nevertheless, except you share
    With them in hell the sorrowful dark of hell,
    Whose world is but the trembling of a flare,
    And heaven but as the highway for a shell,

You shall not hear their mirth:
    You shall not come to think them well content
    By any jest of mine. These men are worth
    Your tears. You are not worth their merriment.

EXPOSURE

Our brains ache, in the merciless iced east winds that
    knive us . . .
Wearied we keep awake because the night is silent . . .
Low, drooping flares confuse our memory of the salient . . .
Worried by silence, sentries whisper, curious, nervous,
        But nothing happens.

Watching, we hear the mad gusts tugging on the wire,
Like twitching agonies of men among its brambles.
Northward, incessantly, the flickering gunnery rumbles,
Far off, like a dull rumour of some other war.
        What are we doing here?

The poignant misery of dawn begins to grow . . .
We only know war lasts, rain soaks, and clouds sag stormy.
Dawn massing in the east her melancholy army
Attacks once more in ranks on shivering ranks of gray,
        But nothing happens.

113

. . . 28

I see the cruel spread Wings black with saints!
Silky my breasts not his, mine, mine to withhold
or tender, tender.
I am sifting, nervous, and bold.
The light is changing. Surrender this loveliness
you cannot make me do. *But* I will. Yes.
What horror, down stormy air,
warps towards me? My threatening promise faints —

. . . 29

torture me, Father, lest not I be thine!
Tribunal terrible & pure, my God,
mercy for him and me.
Faces half-fanged, Christ drives abroad,
and though the crop hopes, Jane is so slipshod
I cry. Evil dissolves, & love, like foam;
that love. Prattle of children powers me home,
my heart claps like the swan's
under a frenzy of *who* love me & who shine.

. . . 10

vellum I palm, and dream. Their forest dies
to greensward, privets, elms & towers, whence
a nightingale is throbbing.
Women sleep sound. I was happy once . .
(Something keeps on not happening; I shrink?)
These minutes all their passions & powers sink
and I am not one chance
for an unknown cry or a flicker of unknown eyes.

. . . 11

Chapped souls ours, by the day Spring's strong winds
  swelled,
Jack's pulpits arched, more glad. The shawl I pinned
flaps like a shooting soul
might in such weather Heaven send.
Succumbing half, in spirit, to a salmon sash
I prod the nerveless novel succotash —
I must be disciplined,
in arms, against that one, and our dissidents, and
  myself.

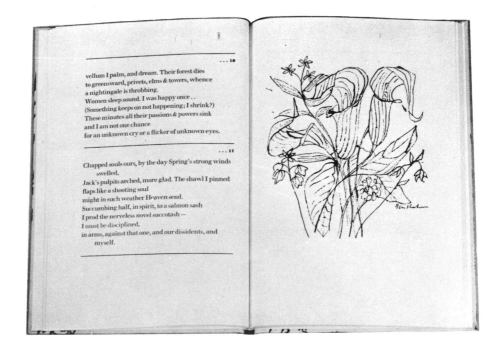

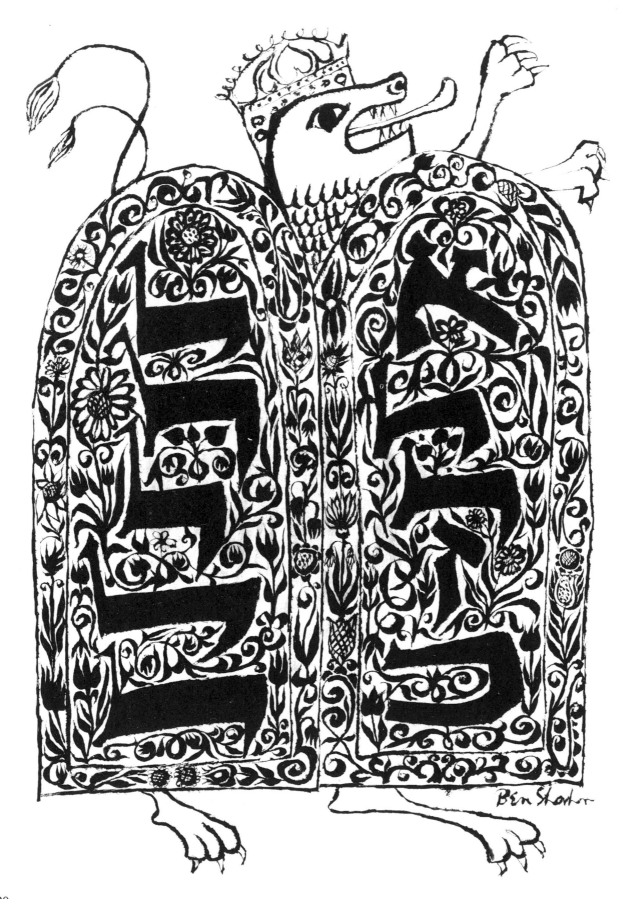

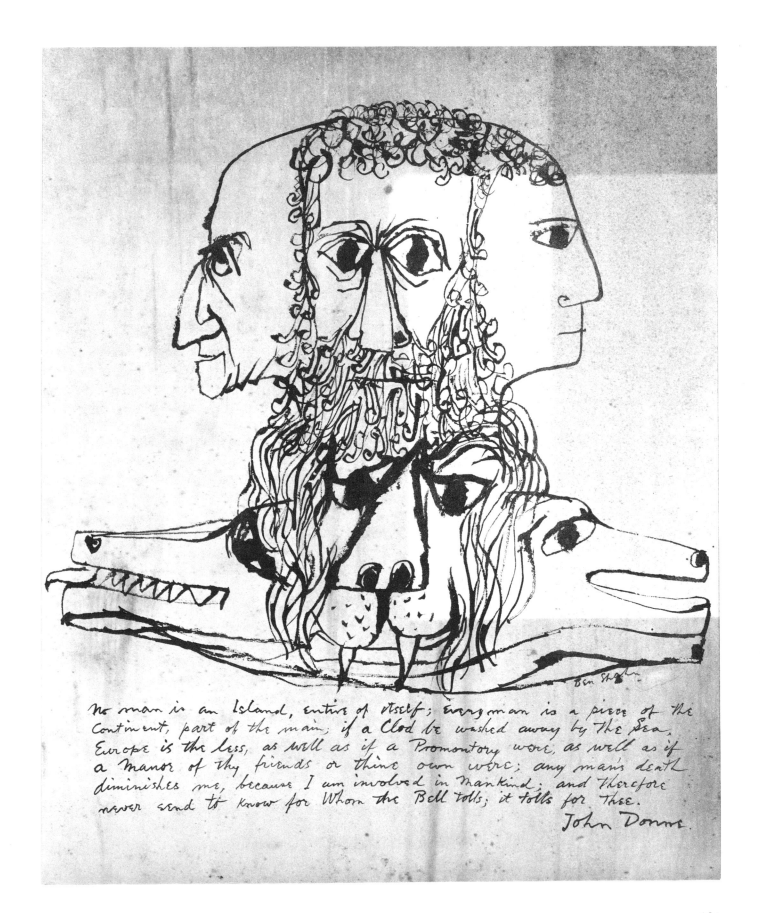

No man is an Island, entire of itself; every man is a piece of the Continent, part of the main; if a Clod be washed away by the Sea, Europe is the less, as well as if a Promontory were, as well as if a Manor of thy friends or thine own were; any man's death diminishes me, because I am involved in Mankind; and therefore never send to know for Whom the Bell tolls; it tolls for Thee.

John Donne.

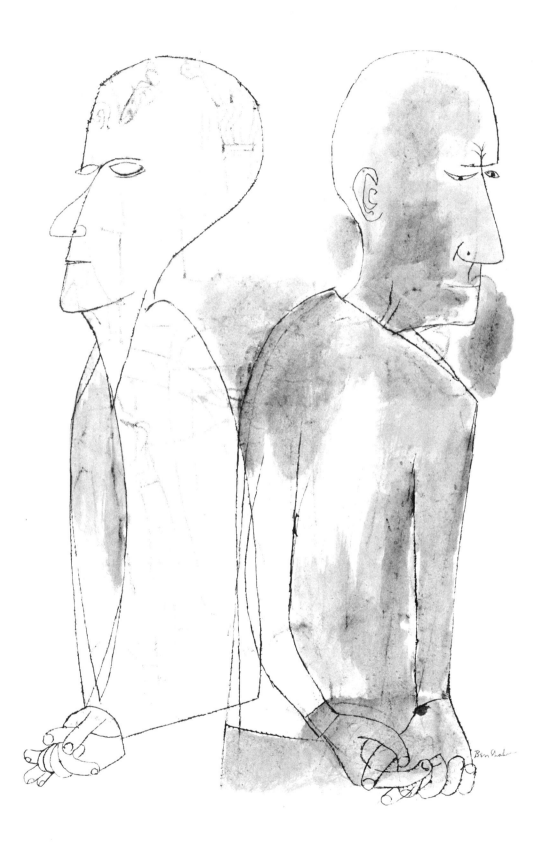

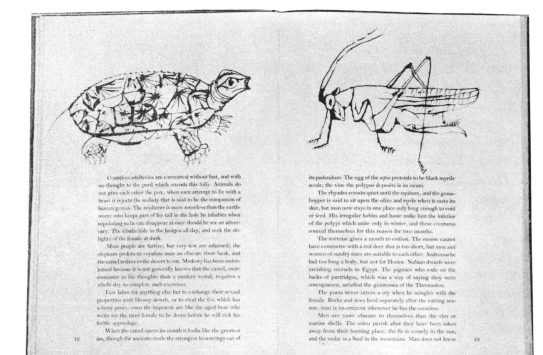

Countless adulteries are committed without lust, and with
no thought to the peril which attends this folly. Animals do
not give each other the pox; when men attempt to lie with a
beast it rejects the malady that is said to be the companion of
human genius. The adulterer is more senseless than the earth-
worm who keeps part of his tail in the hole he inhabits when
copulating so he can disappear at once should he see an adver-
sary. The tibulæ hide in the hedges all day, and seek the de-
lights of the female at dusk.

Most people are furtive, but very few are ashamed; the
elephant prefers to copulate near an obscure river bank, and
the camel retires to the desert to rut. Modesty has been under-
mined because it is not generally known that the camel, more
continent in his thoughts than a modern vestal, requires a
whole day to complete such exercises.

Few labor for anything else but to exchange their sexual
properties with blowsy dowds, or to rival the fox which has
a bony penis; even the impotent are like the aged boar who
waits for the tired female to lie down before he will risk his
feeble appendage.

When the camel opens its mouth it looks like the greatest
ass, though the ancients made the strongest bowstrings out of

12

its pudendum. The egg of the *sepia* pretends to be black myrtle
seeds; the vine the polypus deposits is its ovum.

The rhyades remain quiet until the equinox, and the grass-
hopper is said to sit upon the olive and reeds when it casts its
skin, but man now stays in one place only long enough to void
or feed. His irregular habits and haste make him the inferior
of the polypi which unite only in winter, and these creatures
conceal themselves for this reason for two months.

The tortoise gives a month to coition. The moose cannot
have commerce with a red deer that is too short, but men and
women of sundry sizes are suitable to each other. Andromache
had too long a body, but not for Hector. Nubian dwarfs were
ravishing morsels in Egypt. The pigmies who rode on the
backs of partridges, which was a way of saying they were
concupiscent, satisfied the giantesses of the Thermodon.

The puma never utters a cry when he mingles with the
female. Bucks and does herd separately after the rutting sea-
son; man is incontinent wherever he has the occasion.

Men are more obscure to themselves than the elm or
marine shells. The *ioleos* perish after they have been taken
away from their borning place; the fir is comely in the sun,
and the cedar is a Saul in the mountains. Man does not know

13

tubular siphon of a squid. It is said that man alone has a face,
though if one goes abroad this statement is likely to be denied.

The dolichocephalic head is wonderful to behold, and one
can have some certainties regarding the cranium of a great
faculty. It is easier, however, to recognize the head of a pom-
pion or a gross churl than to discern a wise head. Homer in-
forms us that the head of Thersites is peaked at the top; Thersites employs scurrile words, and is always reviling Odysseus,
or Agamemnon, or Achilles for no other reason than that they
are superior to him in understanding.

There is no greater ruse than the human physiognomy;
the eyes, the nose, and the hands are subtle snares, and the
most practiced observer is not sure whether the genius of the
person is in the general expression of the entire character, or
whether it is to be viewed in the behavior of the neck, or the
shape of the nose. He who relies on the testimony of his eyes
is very likely to be duped. The character of a person is as
much of a riddle as the substance of the soul or the Intelligence
of the Universe. In the Cherubim of Ezekiel the ox in one
cheek is the ruminative side of the face, and the eagle in the
other signifies power. Frequently one sees only the predatory
eagle, for men employ their force for booty rather than as
angels.

There are countenances which at first blush look like wis-
dom, but upon closer acquaintance turn out to be vacant. This
is particularly true of the large proboscis on the face. Most
men of considerable intellectual strength have a conspicuous
nose resembling a potato, a squill, a testiculate cucumber, for
the nose is the second phallus in the male. Besides that, it is
the messenger to the testes, for virile olfactories not only take
much delight in the *Analects* of Socrates or in the *Dialogues* of
Plato, but they also revel in good weather, inhale the seas
and fruits, and are very quick to capture the fragrant skin of
Nicarete of Megara or the adulterous uterus of Clytemnestra.

Agamemnon had a heavy rather than a strong nose, and
he was a coarse rustic soldier with women, for warriors are
not acute in amorous matters, and for this reason was of little
worth to Clytemnestra.

The small nose is regarded as more comely in a man, and
though it is handsome in a face at table, it generally goes with
a short, miserable penis in bed. Lascivious women run after

25

124

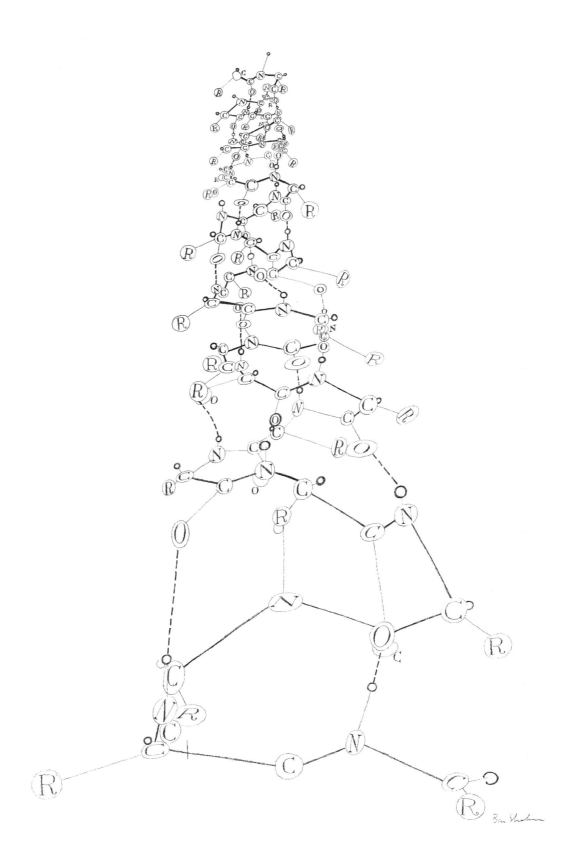

CHRONOLOGY AND BIBLIOGRAPHY

CHRONOLOGY

The Chronology and the Bibliography were prepared by Miss Barbara Novak with the assistance of Mr. Shahn and The Downtown Gallery for The Institute of Contemporary Art, Boston, Mass.

1898   Born Kovno, Lithuania.

1906   To America. Settled with his family in Brooklyn.

1913–17   Attended high school at night. Worked as a lithographer's apprentice by day. Employed on and off at lithography until 1930.

1919–22   Attended New York University and later City College of New York. Received summer scholarships in botany at Woods Hole, 1921, 1922. Left City College in 1922 to study at the National Academy of Design.

1925   Travel abroad: North Africa (Shahn's interest aroused by the art and writings of Eugene Delacroix), Spain, France, Italy.

1927   To Europe again. Second visit to North Africa, especially the Island of Djerba.

1929   Returned to America.

1930   First one-man exhibition at the Downtown Gallery, New York: mostly African subjects. Painted beach scenes at Truro, Mass.

1931–32   Execution of the Sacco-Vanzetti series: 23 gouaches on the trial of Nicola Sacco and Bartolomeo Vanzetti, who were convicted in 1921 of the 1920 murder of a paymaster and his guard, and were executed in 1927.

Drawing (above) commissioned by Edward R. Murrow and Fred W. Friendly for the film "Ambassador Satchmo," 1956, edited by Mili Lerner. 4⅞ x 6. Owned by the artist.

1932   Exhibition of the Sacco-Vanzetti series at the Downtown Gallery, and at the Harvard Society for Contemporary Art, Cambridge, Mass. Two mural panels on the Sacco-Vanzetti theme exhibited at the Museum of Modern Art, New York.

1932–33   Executed 15 gouaches and a tempera panel on the case of Tom Mooney, the labor leader, and exhibited these at the Downtown Gallery. Diego Rivera, the Mexican artist, admired them, and hired Shahn as his assistant on the ill-fated fresco "Man at the Crossroads," commissioned for the RCA Building in Rockefeller Center, New York.

1933–34   Impressed by the exhibition in New York in 1933 of the photographs of Henri Cartier-Bresson. With the encouragement of the American photographer, Walker Evans, took photographs of New York street scenes. Executed a series of 8 temperas on prohibition for a projected mural decoration for the Central Park Casino, under the auspices of the New York City Public Works of Art Project.

1934   Along with Lou Block, commissioned by the Federal Emergency Relief Administration to prepare murals for a prison corridor at Riker's Island Penitentiary, New York.

1935   Murals for Riker's Island rejected by the Municipal Art Commission after sketches were approved by the Mayor and Commissioner of Correction.

1935–38   Employed as artist, designer, and photographer for Farm Security Administration.

1937   Started sketches for a mural, never executed, for a town hall near Milwaukee, Wisconsin, on a theme dealing with the strong liberal and independent political movement in Wisconsin.

1937–38   Executed a single-wall fresco for the community center of a Federal housing development for garment workers at Roosevelt, New Jersey, commissioned by the Farm Security Administration. Shahn himself still lives in the development.

1938–39   With his wife, Bernarda Bryson, executed 13 large mural panels in egg tempera for the main lobby of the Bronx Central Annex Post Office, New York. Commissioned by the Section of Fine Arts, Public Buildings Administration, U.S. Treasury.

1939–40   Executed 9 scale sketches for a series of murals on the Four Freedoms, to be painted in the post office at St. Louis, Missouri, sponsored by the Section of Fine Arts, Public Buildings Administration, U.S. Treasury. Project not accepted. In 1939 executed a mural-size panel in egg tempera on canvas for the Jamaica, Long Island post office, on the theme of the Four Freedoms.

1940–42   Entered and won competition with 375 artists for commission for murals for the main corridor of the Social Security Building (now the Department of Health, Education and Welfare), Washington, D.C., sponsored by the Section of Fine Arts, P.B.A., U.S. Treasury.

1942–43   Designed posters for the Office of War Information. Only two posters published.

1943–
to the
present   Commercial commissions for Container Corporation of America, Columbia Broadcasting System, Columbia Records, Fortune, Time, Charm, Seventeen, Esquire, Harper's, Scientific American, Vintage Books, and others.

1944–46   Chief artist for the Political Action Committee of the Congress of Industrial Organizations. Executed posters for this group.

1947   Taught at Boston Museum Summer School, Pittsfield, Mass. Retrospective exhibition of 16 paintings at the Mayor Gallery, London, under the auspices of the Arts Council of Great Britain.

1947–48   Retrospective exhibition of paintings, drawings, posters, illustrations, and photographs at the Museum of Modern Art, New York.

1948   Chosen one of "Ten Best Painters" in the Look Magazine poll. Posters and campaign material for the Henry Wallace "Third Party" movement.

1949   Lectured for a week at the University of Wisconsin.

1950   Taught for ten weeks at the University of Colorado Summer Session in Boulder, Colorado.

1951   Taught at the Brooklyn Museum Art School.

1952   Attended the Democratic National Convention and did drawings on the scene.

1954   Won the $800 award offered by the Museum of Sao Paulo, Brazil. Chosen along with Willem De Kooning to represent American painting at the Venice Biennale.

1955   Twenty-fifth anniversary exhibition of paintings and drawings at the Downtown Gallery, New York (marking 25 years of association with the gallery).

1956   Won the Joseph E. Temple Gold Medal Award at the Pennsylvania Academy. Trip to Europe.

1956–57   Named Charles Eliot Norton Professor of Poetry at Harvard University. Mosaic for William E. Grady Vocational High School in

Brooklyn, New York, commissioned by New York City Board of Education.

Retrospective exhibition of Shahn's work at the Fogg Art Museum, Cambridge, Mass.

1957   Documentary exhibition surveying separate aspects of Shahn's work, at the Institute of Contemporary Art, Boston, Mass.

BIBLIOGRAPHY

ABBREVIATIONS

The form of the bibliography is modeled upon that used by the Art Index. For example, the first article cited, *Angry Eye,* appeared in Volume 50 of Time Magazine, on page 63, in the issue of October 13, 1947, and was an illustrated article.

Ag	August	Ja	January	N	November
Ap	April	Je	June	no.	number(s)
D	December	Jy	July	O	October
F	February	Mr	March	p	page(s)
il	illustration(s)	My	May	S	September

1. About the Artist

BOOKS

RODMAN, SELDEN. *Portrait of the Artist as an American. Ben Shahn: A Biography with Pictures.* Harper & Bros., New York, 1951.

SOBY, JAMES THRALL. *Ben Shahn.* Penguin Modern Painters. Penguin Books, Middlesex, England, 1947.

ARTICLES

"Angry Eye." *Time* 50:63 O 13 '47 il.

"A Tempera and a Drawing by Ben Shahn." *University of Michigan Bulletin* 1951, vol. 1 no. 2 My '51.

"Baffling Ben." *Time* 58:82 N 5 '51 il.

"Ben Shahn a Venezia." *Domus* no. 298:36–37 S '54 il.

Drawing (above) commissioned by
Edward R. Murrow and Fred W.
Friendly for the film "Ambassador
Satchmo," 1956, edited by Mili Lerner.
6 x 9⅝. Owned by the artist.

Ben Shahn: Downtown Gallery. *Art News* 31:5 My 13 '33. Review.

"Ben Shahn: Painter of Protest Turns to Reflection." *Life* 37:96–100 O 4 '54 il.

"Ben Shahn. Portrait of the Artist no. 182." *Art News and Review.* Vol. 7 no. 26:1 Ja '56.

Ben Shahn's "The Third Allegory" added to the Center's Permanent Collection. *Jewish Center News,* Buffalo. Ap '56.

"Bitterness Leavened with Wit." *Art Digest* 24:12 N 1 '49 il. Review of exhibition.

BREUNING, MARGARET. "Ben Shahn Looks Upon the Seamy Side." *Art Digest* 19:17 D 1 '44 il. Review.

"The Bronx—A Typical Treasury Competition." *Art Digest* 12:26 Je 1 '38 il.

BRYSON, BERNARDA. "The Drawings of Ben Shahn." *Image,* London, no. 2 Autumn '49 p 31–50 il.

CHAMBERLAIN, BETTY. "Ben Shahn at the Museum of Modern Art." *Art News* 46:40–1 O '47 il.

CHARLOT, JEAN. "Ben Shahn." *Hound and Horn* 6 no. 4:632–4 Jy–S '33 il. Text reprinted with 4 plates omitted in *Art from the Mayans to Disney* p 189–92, Sheed & Ward, New York, 1939.

CHARLOT, JEAN. "Murals for Tomorrow." *Art News* 44:20–3 Jy '45 il.

COATES, ROBERT M. "New Show at the Downtown Gallery." *The New Yorker* 20:95 D 2 '44.

COATES, ROBERT M. "Contemporary Americans." *The New Yorker* 23:64 O 11 '47.

COATES, ROBERT M. "Ben Shahn. Exhibition of Paintings and Drawings at the Downtown Gallery." *The New Yorker* 25:79–80 N 5 '49.

COATES, ROBERT M. "Exhibition at the Downtown Gallery." *The New Yorker* 30:54 Ja 29 '55.

CONTAINER CORPORATION OF AMERICA. "Modern Art in Advertising: Designs for Container Corporation of America." Chicago, Paul Theobald, 1946 il.

DAVIS, STUART. "We Reject—The Art Commission." *Art Front* 1 no. 6:4–5 Jy '35 il.

Designs from the Alphabet of Creation. *Print* 9:cover 14 O '54.

Downtown Gallery. Sacco-Vanzetti Series. *Creative Art* 10:396 My '32. *Art News* 30:10 Ap 9 '32. Reviews.

ELIOT, ALEXANDER. "Under the Four Winds." Art Exhibition in Venice. *Time* 63:74 Je 28 '54 il.

Empty Tennis Court. Illustration for *Seventeen*. *Print* 10:22 S '55.

Exhibition of Tempera and Drawings at the Downtown Gallery. *Art News* 48:44 N '49 il. Review.

Exhibition. Downtown Gallery. *Art News* 51:45 Ap '52. Review.

Exhibition of Drawings at the Downtown Gallery. *Art Digest* 25:19 Je '51 il. Review.

Exhibition of Drawings in Color and Black and White at the Downtown Gallery. *Art News* 50:47 Je '51 il. Review.

"Five Painters of America." *Worcester Museum News Bulletin* 20:21–4, Sup 1–4, Mr '55 il.

GREENBERG, CLEMENT. "Art." *The Nation* 165:481 N 1 '47.

GUTMAN, WALTER. "The Passion of Sacco-Vanzetti." *The Nation* 134:475 Ap 20 '32. Review.

HARLING, ROBERT. "Ben Shahn in Roosevelt." *Art* vol. 1 no. 15:2–3 Je 9 '55 il.

"Heard at the Galleries." *Pictures on Exhibit* 6:16 N '44. Review.

HESS, THOMAS B. "Ben Shahn Paints a Picture: Nocturne." *Art News* 48:20–2 My '49 il.

HUXTABLE, ADA LOUISE. "Designed to Sell." Exhibition at the Museum of Modern Art. *Art Digest* 29:12 Mr 1 '54.

JOSEPHSON, MATTHEW. "Passion of Sacco-Vanzetti." *New Republic* 70 no. 907:275 Ap 20 '32.

LANE, JAMES W. "New Pictures by Shahn; Theodore Lux." *Art News* 38:11 My 18 '40. Review of Julien Levy Exhibition.

LERMAN, LEO. "American Eye." *House and Garden* 90:209 D '46.

The Living Theatre. "Sharecroppers . . . seen by the camera eye of Dorothea Lange and Ben Shahn." *Theatre & Film* 4 no. 11:24–5 Ap '37 il.

LIONNI, LEO. "Ben Shahn, His Graphic Work." *Graphis* 11 no. 62:468–485 '55 il.

LOUCHHEIM, ALINE B. "Shahn Feels Deeply and Sees Clearly." *Art News* 43:18–19 N 15 '44 il.

Made Charles Eliot Norton Professor at Harvard for Next Year. *Art News* 55:7 Je '56.

"Mirrors and Messages." Retrospective Exhibition at the Downtown Gallery. *Time* 65:60 Ja 31 '55 il. Review.

"Modern Museum Honors Ben Shahn." *Art Digest* 22:11 O 15 '47 il. Review.

MOE, OLE HENRICK. "Ben Shahn." *Kunsten Idag* vol. 35 no. 1:30–52 '56; p 56–8 English text. il.

"Mooney Theme." *Art Digest* 7:14 My 1 '33. Review.

"Morals in Murals." *Art Front* 1 no. 6:3 Jy '35.

Museum of Modern Art's Circulating Exhibition. *Baltimore Museum News* 11:6 Ap '48.

Named Charles Eliot Norton Professor at Harvard University for 1956–57. *Arts* 30:8 Je '56.

New Tempera and Watercolor Paintings at Downtown Gallery. *Art Digest* 26:20 Ap 1 '52. Review.

"1955 Jury of Award for the 1955 Pittsburgh International." *Carnegie Magazine* 29:262 O '55.

"Ohio Magic" acquired by Museum. *California Palace of the Legion of Honor Bulletin* 6:72 D '48 il.

PARIS, GEORGE. "Ben Shahn." *Motive* p 11–16 Mr '50.

PEARSON, R. M. "Ben Shahn at the Modern." *Art Digest* 22:36 D 1 '47.

Portrait. *Art Digest* 28:3 N 1 '53.

Portrait. *Art News* 46:36 Ja '48.

Portrait. *Art News* 48:13 Ja '50.

Portrait of the Artist as an American. "Ben Shahn" by Selden Rodman. *Art Digest* 26:22 D 1 '51. *Magazine of Art* 46:43 Ja '53. Reviews.

Retrospective Exhibition at the Downtown Gallery. *Art News* 53:56 F '55 il. Review.

RODMAN, SELDEN. "Ben Shahn." Portfolio, Cincinnati, 1951.

RODMAN, SELDEN. "Ben Shahn: Painter of America." *Perspectives USA* no. 1:87–96 Fall '52 il.

Sacco-Vanzetti Series. *Art Digest* 6:31 Ap 15 '32.

Scenes from the Living Theatre—Sidewalks of New York: photographs by Ben Shahn. *New Theatre* 1 no. 10:18–19 N '34.

Shahn/Baskin: Collaboration on the Color Wood Engraving: Beatitudes. *Art News* 54:17 N '55 il.

"Shahn Best of 375." Mural Competition for the Social Security Building. *Art Digest* 15:8 N 15 '40.

SOBY, JAMES THRALL. "Ben Shahn." German and French texts. *Graphis* 4 no. 22:102–7 '48 il.

Soby, James Thrall. "Ben Shahn and Morris Graves." *Horizon,* London, no. 93–4:48–57 O '47 il.

Soby, James Thrall. "Ben Shahn and Morris Graves." *Contemporary Painters,* Museum of Modern Art, New York, 1948, p 40–50.

Special Issue Devoted to the Retrospective Shahn Exhibition; with chronology, list of previous exhibitions, and catalogue. *Museum of Modern Art Bulletin,* 14 no. 4–5:1–47 Summer '47 il.

"Spring" acquired by the Gallery. *Gallery Notes,* Buffalo, 12 no. 3:26 '48 il.

Stokes, I. N. Phelps. Letter to the editor protesting Whiting's article. *American Magazine of Art* 28:635–7 O '35.

Three Paintings for *Charm* Fiction. *Print* 10:24 S '55 il.

Twenty-five Years of Shahn's Work at the Downtown Gallery. *Art Digest* 29:22 F 1 '55 il. Review.

U.S. Works Projects Administration. *The Ohio Guide,* compiled by members of the Writers' program . . . Oxford University Press, N.Y. 1940 (American Guide series). Photos by Shahn are included.

Whiting, Philippa. "Speaking about Art: Riker's Island." *American Magazine of Art* 28 no. 8:492–6 Ag '35 il.

"Whitman Censored." Protest against the mural decoration for Bronx Post Office. *Art Digest* 13:14 Ja 1 '39.

Woolfenden, William E. "Composition for Clarinets and Tin Horn." *Detroit Institute of Arts Bulletin* 32 no. 1:20–1 '52–53 il.

EXHIBITION CATALOGUES

1930   Downtown Gallery, April 8–27.
        Ben Shahn. Paintings and Drawings.

1932   Downtown Gallery, April 5–17.
        The Passion of Sacco-Vanzetti.

        Harvard Society of Contemporary Art, October 17–29.
        Exhibition of the passion of Sacco-Vanzetti and the Dreyfus case.

1933   Downtown Gallery, May 2–20, introduction by Diego Rivera.
        The Mooney Case.

1944   Downtown Gallery, November 14–December 2.
        Shahn paintings.

1947   Arts Council of Great Britain. Mayor Gallery, London, May, 1947.
        Ben Shahn. (16 paintings)

1947–48   MUSEUM OF MODERN ART, NEW YORK, September 30, 1947–January 4, 1948. Bulletin: Vol. XIV, 4–5, 1947.
Ben Shahn. Retrospective exhibition of paintings, drawings, posters, illustrations and photographs.

1949   DOWNTOWN GALLERY, October 25–November 12.
Ben Shahn. New Paintings and Drawings.

1950   THE LITTLE GALLERY OF THE ALBRIGHT ART SCHOOL, March 17–April 27.
Ben Shahn. Drawings.

1951   THE ARTS CLUB OF CHICAGO, October 2–27.
Ben Shahn, Willem De Kooning, Jackson Pollock.

1952   DOWNTOWN GALLERY, March 11–29.
Ben Shahn. Paintings.

SANTA BARBARA MUSEUM OF ART, CALIFORNIA PALACE OF THE LEGION OF HONOR, LOS ANGELES COUNTY MUSEUM, June–August.
Paintings by Lee Gatch, Karl Knaths, Ben Shahn.

1954   CONTEMPORARY ARTS MUSEUM, HOUSTON, January 10–February 11.
Four Americans from the Real to the Abstract.

DETROIT INSTITUTE OF ARTS, March 9–April 11.
Ben Shahn, Charles Sheeler, Joe Jones.

RENAISSANCE SOCIETY AT THE UNIVERSITY OF CHICAGO, November 6–20.
Ben Shahn. 8 silkscreen prints, 2 drawings.

ALLYN ART GALLERY, Southern Illinois University, November 1–24.
Ben Shahn. Drawings and serigraphs.

XXVII BIENNALE VENEZIA, 1954, Stati Uniti d'America.
2 pittori: De Kooning, Shahn; 3 scultori: Lachaise, Lassaw, Smith.

1955   DOWNTOWN GALLERY, January 18–February 12.
Ben Shahn. Exhibition of Paintings and Drawings. Twenty-fifth anniversary of the artist's association with the Downtown Gallery.

1956–57   FOGG ART MUSEUM, HARVARD UNIVERSITY, December 4, 1956–January 19, 1957.
The Art of Ben Shahn.

AMERICAN INSTITUTE OF GRAPHIC ARTS, N.Y., March 1–28.
The Graphic Works of Ben Shahn. Mainly material as reproduced for commercial commissions, with a few originals. Checklist issued.

2. By the Artist

BOOKS

Paragraphs on Art. Spiral Press, New York, 1952.

The Biography of a Painting, Fogg Picture Book No. 6. Fogg Museum, Harvard University, 1956.

To be published in spring, 1958, by Harvard University Press: The Charles Eliot Norton Lectures 1956–7.

ARTICLES

"An Artist's Credo." *College Art Journal* 9 no. 1:43–5 '49.

"Aspects of the Art of Paul Klee." *Museum of Modern Art Bulletin* 17 no. 4:6–9 '50.

"Ben Shahn: An Interview." Shahn quoted by JOHN D. MORSE. *Magazine of Art* 37:136–41 Ap '44.

"Ben Shahn Speaking." Edited by SELDEN RODMAN. *Perspectives USA* p 59–72 Ja '52.

"Henri Cartier-Bresson." JOHN D. MORSE. Includes Shahn quotes. *Magazine of Art* 40:189 My '47.

"How an Artist Looks at Aesthetics." *Journal of Aesthetics and Art Criticism* 13:46–51 S '54.

"How to Combine Architecture, Painting and Sculpture." (Published report of a symposium: The Relation of Painting and Sculpture to Architecture, held at the Museum of Modern Art Mr 19 '51.) *Interiors* 110:102 My '51.

"Paragraphs on Art." *Graphis* 11 no. 62:468–85 '55.

"Photos for Art." Includes commentary by Ben Shahn. *U.S. Camera* 9 no. 4:30–2, 57 My '46.

"Political Cartoons Today." *Art News* 53:50 O '54.

Statement by the Artist. Catalogue of exhibition: *American Realists and Magic Realists.* Museum of Modern Art, N.Y. 1943, p 52–3.

"The Artist and the Politicians." *Art News* 52:34–5 S '53; *Rights* 1 no. 1 My '53.

"The Artist's Point of View." *Magazine of Art* 42:266 N '49.

"The Future of the Creative Arts." Symposium. *University of Buffalo Studies* 19 no. 4:125–8 F '52.

"What is Realism in Art." *Look* 16:44–5 Ja 13 '53.

The text and notes for this book were photomechanically composed by Graphic Services, Inc.; black and white illustrations printed by Herst Litho, Inc.; color illustrations by Triggs Color Printing Corp.; endpapers printed by Philip Klein; bound by The Haddon Craftsmen, Inc.; book design and layout by T. E. Mergendahl Jr.